1 はじめに

　2017–2021 年にアメリカの大統領を務めたドナルド・トランプ氏 (Donald John Trump, 1946 年 6 月 14 日生まれ) は、再選を逃したものの 2024 年の大統領選で共和党の最有力候補として再び注目を集めています．

　歴代のアメリカの大統領に関して，彼らの発言が後世にまで残る名言とされて伝わっています．有名なものですと，例えば第 16 代大統領 Abraham Lincoln のゲティスバーグでの演説 "... that government of the people, by the people, for the people ..." (人民の人民による，人民のための政治) です．彼は
"With malice toward none, with charity for all." (誰にも悪意を持たず，全ての人に愛を)
という名言をも遺しています．

　さて，トランプ氏は誰にでもわかりやすいスピーチばかりしています．基本方針は「アメリカ第一主義」「偉大なアメリカの復活」です．トランプ氏のスピーチの語彙は小学生レベルとも言えそうです．ただ，これはスピーチが誰にでもわかりやすいように簡単な表現しか使わず，大衆の心を掴んだとも言えるでしょう．

　政財界の要人の言動は「ポリティカル・コレクトネス」[*1]に注意が払われます．ところがトランプ氏の言動はそのようなことがお構い無しのように見えます．ポリティカル・コレクトネスを考えず，自由気ままに発言することが支持されたという見方もあります．

　そこでトランプ氏の大統領就任までの発言や Twitter での tweet，さらには物議を醸したオフレコの発言に注目して，トランプ氏の英語表現を学んでみましょう[*2]．

2 公式サイト

　トランプ氏の公式サイトは
https://www.donaldjtrump.com/
です．ここでは文体が整えられた主張や，メディアで取り上げられた発言，動向が整理されています．大げさな言動や過激な発言はメディアがこぞって取り上げるため，広告を自分から進んで行わなくても広まるという点を利用したと思われます．

[*1] 人種・宗教・性別などの違いによる偏見・差別を含まない，中立的な表現や用語を用いること．米国で，偏見・差別のない表現は政治的に妥当である，という意味で使われるようになった．言葉の問題にとどまらず，社会から偏見・差別をなくすことを意味する場合もある．ポリティカリーコレクト．PC．政治的妥当性．(出典：デジタル大辞泉)

[*2] 彼の表現をビジネスの場や学会発表などで使うと，非常に無礼で大きな損失を被ることがあります．せいぜい，友人同士の会話にとどめておくのが無難かと思われます．

トランプ氏の主張がまとまっている報道として，例えば 2016 年 4 月 4 日の FOX News が挙げられます[3]．

もちろん，発言そのものもまとまって掲載されています．2016 年 4 月 27 日の外交政策に関する発言[4] を取り上げてみます．

America First will be the major and overriding theme of my administration.
But to chart our path forward, we must first briefly look back.
We have a lot to be proud of. In the 1940s we saved the world. The Greatest Generation beat back the Nazis and the Japanese Imperialists.

「アメリカ第一主義」を掲げて歴史を振り返るのですが，第二次世界大戦でナチスと日本帝国主義者 (Imperialists) を打ち負かした (beat back) というところから振り返るのは，なんとも複雑な気持ちになります．その後，冷戦で全体主義の共産主義に勝ったことを挙げますが，冷戦後の外交を見誤り，イラク，エジプト，シリアで失敗を犯したことを挙げています．そして ISIS がはびこることになったため，オバマ大統領の方針をこき下ろしています．

Our foreign policy is a complete and total disaster.
No vision, no purpose, no direction, no strategy.

アメリカの外交方針が完全な惨事であり，ビジョンも目的も方向性も戦略もないと批判しているわけです．この後に外交方針において，5 つの主要な弱点を挙げています．

発言の締めくくりは，後述の Twitter で盛んに繰り返されるフレーズです．

We must make America respected again. And we must make America great again.
If we do that, perhaps this century can be the most peaceful and prosperous the world has ever known. Thank you.

3 遊説中の発言

トランプ氏の選挙活動は，まずは注目を集めることに重点が置かれたようです．注目されることで様々なメディアが取り上げるため，広告費をかけずに大きな宣伝ができるということです．

例えば日本の核武装に関する発言を 2016 年 6 月にしています．これは日本でも大きく取り上げられたので記憶している方も多いでしょう．

---

[3] https://www.donaldjtrump.com/media/
  trump-doubles-down-on-allies-paying-more-for-us-protection-vows-to-rep
  eal-o
[4] https://www.donaldjtrump.com/press-releases/donald-j.-trump-foreign-pol
  icy-speech

トランプ氏に学ぶ英語表現！

暗黒通信団

Clinton made a speech, she's making another one tomorrow, and they sent me a copy of the speech. And it was such lies about my foreign policy, that they said I want Japan to get nuclear weapons. Give me a break.

See they don't say it: I want Japan and Germany and Saudi Arabia and South Korea and many of the NATO states, nations, they owe us tremendously, we're taking care of all those people and what I want them to do is pay up.

次の章で詳細を述べますが，トランプ氏は Twitter での発言を多用しています．選挙に勝った後の tweet で，上記の発言はしておらず New York Times は嘘つきと断じています．

The @nytimes states today that DJT believes "more countries should acquire nuclear weapons." How dishonest are they. I never said this! (8:03 - 2016 年 11 月 13 日)

10 月になり，ヒラリー・クリントン氏の国防長官の業務メールを私用メールアカウントでやりとりしていた件についても，はっきりと攻撃しています．

I need to open with a very critical breaking news announcement. The FBI has just sent a letter to Congress informing them that they have discovered new emails pertaining to former Secretary of State Hillary Clinton's investigation, and they are reopening the case into her criminal and illegal conduct that threatens the security of the United States of America.

Hillary Clinton's corruption is on a scale we have never seen before. We must not let her take her criminal scheme into the Oval Office.

I have great respect for the fact that the FBI and the DOJ are now willing to have the courage to right the horrible mistake that they made. This was a grave miscarriage of justice that the American people fully understand. It is everybody's hope that it is about to be corrected.

"the Oval Office" は大統領執務室です．こんな腐敗は前例がなく，犯罪計画を大統領執務室に持ち込むべきではないとしています．

遊説の締めくくりはミシガン州で投票前日に行われました．自動車産業発祥の州として知られる州ですが，自動車産業の不振によりいわゆる「ビッグ 3」が次々に経営危機に陥ってしまいました．このため，失業率は全米トップレベル，州都デトロイトは犯罪発生率が高くなっています．このような場所で，自身への支持を呼びかけたというところが，選挙の勝因の一つと考えられます．

After we win, I'm going to be coming back to Michigan a lot. I'm going to be coming back every time we open a new factory or a new automobile plant, and we're going to be doing a lot of expansion. I know exactly what to do folks. We are going

3

to bring back the automobile industry to Michigan, bigger and better and stronger than before.

Now we have one flawed candidate left to beat. It's going to be the very beginning of a new adventure ... it's making America great again, we're going to do it. Michigan now stands at the crossroads of history. If we win Michigan, we will win this historic election and then we will be able to do all the things that we have wanted to do.

新たな工場や自動車プラントを建設し，かつてのようなミシガンに自動車産業を戻すとまで宣言しています．雇用を拡大するということです．そしてミシガンで勝てば，歴史的な選挙に勝つことになり，望むものは全て叶うとまで言い切っています．最終日とはいえ，かなり強気な発言と言えるでしょう．

4 Twitter での数々の tweet

トランプ氏は Twitter での発言を多用してきました．彼の公式 Twitter のアカウントは

https://twitter.com/realdonaldtrump

です．「ワンフレーズ」で有権者に訴えかけるトランプ氏にとって，短文を拡散するTwitter は非常に強力な武器となったことでしょう．Twitter で以下の発言はいずれも数万件もの「いいね」がつけられているものがほとんどです．まず，2012 年の時点でこのようなことをつぶやいています．

My twitter has become so powerful that I can actually make my enemies tell the truth. (8:06 - 2012 年 10 月 17 日)

中学校や高校の英文で頻出の "so ... that" 構文ですが，中身は如何でしょうか．「敵に本当のことを言わせる」というのは，大統領選でいかがでしたか．

まずは「アメリカ第一主義」から見てみましょう．

AMERICA FIRST! (5:28 - 2016 年 6 月 14 日)

Install the official America First app to get the latest campaign news, events and more! Connect with Trump supporters and earn points NOW! (15:20 - 2016 年 10 月 10 日)

Download the official America First app to get the latest campaign news, events and more! (15:27 - 2016 年 10 月 10 日)

Install the America First Connect with other Trump supporters and earn points for taking action to help Make America Great Again! (15:41 - 2016 年 10 月 10 日)

"Make America great again." （アメリカを再び偉大にしよう）ということも繰り返

しています．トランプ氏の tweet で頻出のフレーズです．オバマ大統領が "Yes we can." を繰り返していたように，トランプ氏の決まり文句のようです．

Nation's infrastructure is collapsing, MAKE AMERICA GREAT AGAIN! (16:02 - 2013 年 5 月 25 日) *It's this simple. "Make America Great Again." #debate #BigLeagueTruth* (18:11 - 2016 年 10 月 9 日) *MAKE AMERICA GREAT AGAIN!* (6:33 - 2016 年 11 月 5 日) *TODAY WE MAKE AMERICA GREAT AGAIN!* (3:43 - 2016 年 11 月 8 日)

選挙間近になると大文字での強調を繰り返しています．今回の選挙で自信への支持を訴えかけたのは，かつては盛況でしたが今は不況に陥り，中産階級から没落していった人々と分析されています．その人たちに対し，前述のミシガンでの演説のように支持を取り付けていったと考えられます．

大統領選が近づくにつれて過激さは収束していきましたが，それまでの発言は過激なもののオンパレードです．例としていくつか見てみます．

An 'extremely credible source' has called my office and told me that @BarackObama's birth certificate is a fraud. (13:23 - 2012 年 8 月 6 日)

オバマ大統領の出生証明書 "birth certificate" が偽物 "fraud" とつぶやいています．その後，オバマ大統領がハワイ生まれである出生証明書を公開して，トランプ氏は謝罪する羽目になりました．

その後，メキシコからの不法移民に対する発言でも物議を醸しています．

We must build a great wall between Mexico and the United States! (14:49 - 2016 年 4 月 1 日)

Mexico will pay for the wall! (3:31 - 2016 年 9 月 1 日)

"great wall" は「万里の長城」です．非常にわかりやすいですね[5]．その前からの発言もなかなか過激です．英語表現として，強調したいところを全て大文字にするのは常套手段です．

The Mexican legal system is corrupt, as is much of Mexico. Pay me the money that is owed me now - and stop sending criminals over our border. (16:47 - 2015 年 2 月 24 日)

Druggies, drug dealers, rapists and killers are coming across the southern border. When will the U.S. get smart and stop this travesty? (19:22 - 2015 年 6 月 19 日)

Mexican gov doesn't want me talking about terrible border situation & horrible trade deals. Forcing Univision to get me to stop- no way! (7:26 - 2015 年 6 月 25 日)

---

[5] トランプ氏の「万里の長城」構想については
https://assets.donaldjtrump.com/Pay_for_the_Wall.pdf
に詳しく述べられています．

I love the Mexican people, but Mexico is not our friend. They're killing us at the border and they're killing us on jobs and trade. FIGHT! (5:57 - 2015 年 6 月 30 日)

Again, illegal immigrant is charged with the fatal bludgeoning of a wonderful and loved 64 year old woman. Get them out and build a WALL! (17:29 - 2015 年 8 月 10 日)

2 番目の文章がちょっと難解ですが，"druggies" は「麻薬常習者」の複数形，"travesty" は「戯画化，こじつけ」です．"bludgeoning" は「棍棒」です．移民政策についての詳細は 10 のポイントを挙げています[*6]．Web サイトでは Twitter ほどくだけた表現ではありませんが，オバマ大統領の比較的寛容な政策を否定し，「キャッチアンドリリースをやめる．つまり違法に入国したら拘留する」「聖域とする都市をやめる」「不法移民の雇用に関する厳罰化」などを掲げています．

Well, Obama refused to say (he just can't say it), that we are at WAR with RADICAL ISLAMIC TERRORISTS. (17:45 - 2015 年 12 月 6 日)

I refuse to call Megyn Kelly a bimbo, because that would not be politically correct. Instead I will only call her a lightweight reporter! (3:44 - 2016 年 1 月 27 日)

ここで現れる "bimbo" は，英語ではなかなか使われない単語です．日本語の「貧乏」とは意味が異なり，「美人だが頭のからっぽの女」と言う意味です．Megyn Kelly 氏は FOX ニュースの看板ニュースキャスターの女性です[*7]．

環太平洋パートナーシップ協定 (TPP) について，基本的には反対の意向です．アメリカ以外の国を利するものとしています．

The Trans-Pacific Partnership is an attack on America's business. It does not stop Japan's currency manipulation. This is a bad deal. (13:56 - 2015 年 4 月 22 日)

The Trans-Pacific Partnership will lead to even greater unemployment. Do not pass it. (14:00 - 2015 年 4 月 22 日)

The Trans-Pacific Partnership will increase our trade deficits & send even more jobs overseas. This is a bad deal. Time for smart trade! (8:50 - 2015 年 6 月 3 日)

NAFTA（北米自由貿易協定）を，1992 年に George H. W. Bush 大統領が署名，1994 年にビル・クリントン大統領の施政下で発効したことを批判しています．

Gov Kasich voted for NAFTA, which devastated Ohio and is now pushing TPP hard- bad for American workers! (9:59 - 2016 年 3 月 14 日)

A vote for Clinton-Kaine is a vote for TPP, NAFTA, high taxes, radical regulation, and massive influx of refugees. (13:31 - 2016 年 7 月 28 日)

Word is that Crooked Hillary has very small and unenthusiastic crowds in Penn-

---

[*6] https://www.donaldjtrump.com/policies/immigration/

[*7] http://www.foxnews.com/person/k/megyn-kelly.html

sylvania. Perhaps it is because her husband signed NAFTA? (14:51 - 2016 年 7 月
30 日)

Hillary is too weak to lead on border security-no solutions, no ideas, no credibility.
She supported NAFTA, worst deal in US history. *#Debate* (18:28 - 2016 年 10 月
19 日)

I will renegotiate NAFTA. If I can't make a great deal, we're going to tear it up.
We're going to get this economy running again. *#Debate* (18:45 - 2016 年 10 月
19 日)

日本に対しても，第二次大戦について取り上げた発言が見られます．

Does President Obama ever discuss the sneak attack on Pearl Harbor while he's
in Japan? Thousands of American lives lost. *#MDW* (14:34 - 2016 年 5 月 28 日)

地球温暖化対策としてパリ協定をどうするのか先進国，開発途上国間で議論が盛んにな
されていますが，トランプ氏が次期大統領に就任することが決まり，先進国首脳が説得に
回るという報道も出ています．

The concept of global warming was created by and for the Chinese in order to
make U.S. manufacturing non-competitive. (11:15 - 2012 年 11 月 6 日)

This very expensive GLOBAL WARMING bullshit has got to stop. Our planet is
freezing, record low temps,and our GW scientists are stuck in ice (16:39 - 2014 年 1
月 1 日)

"bullshit" は「たわごと，でたらめ」です．

The global warming we should be worried about is the global warming caused by
NUCLEAR WEAPONS in the hands of crazy or incompetent leaders! (20:53 - 2014
年 5 月 7 日)

Where the hell is global warming when you need it? (15:18 - 2015 年 1 月 26 日)

これだけの発言を繰り返したため，先進国の首脳たちが対応に追われる訳です．

オバマケアについても一貫して廃止を主張してきました．

We may get out of ObamaCare because the train wreck is impossible to implement
http://wapo.st/16EziTr It is a disaster. (12:24 - 2013 年 5 月 20 日)

Obamacare premiums continue to rise and bend up the cross curve. And the
back-end of the website does not even work. (7:03 - 2014 年 10 月 8 日)

Obamacare is a disaster. Rates going through the sky - ready to explode. I will
fix it. Hillary can't! *#ObamacareFailed* (13:43 - 2016 年 10 月 25 日)

Obamacare is a disaster! Time to repeal & replace! *#ObamacareFail* (8:22 - 2016
年 10 月 25 日)

Obamacare is a disaster - as I've been saying from the beginning. Time to repeal

& replace! #ObamacareFail (9:20 - 2016 年 10 月 25 日)

Obamacare is a disaster. We must REPEAL & REPLACE. Tired of the lies, and want to #DrainTheSwamp? Get out & VOTE #TrumpPence16 & lets #MAGA! (5:17 - 2016 年 10 月 27 日)

ObamaCare is a total disaster. Hillary Clinton wants to save it by making it even more expensive. Doesn't work, I will REPEAL AND REPLACE! (5:34 - 2016 年 11 月 3 日)

もちろん過激な発言ばかりではなく，恩人への感謝の気持ちも忘れません．ここでも彼らしい，同じ単語の繰り返し，大文字での強調が見られます．

Governor John Kasich of the GREAT, GREAT, GREAT State of Ohio called to congratulate me on the win. The people of Ohio were incredible! (7:28 - 2016 年 11 月 13 日)

Jeb Bush, George W and George H.W. all called to express their best wishes on the win. Very nice! (7:23 - 2016 年 11 月 13 日)

当然のことながら，対立候補であるヒラリー・クリントン氏に対する批判も多いです．特に国防長官として執務中に，公務のメールを私用メールアカウントでやりとりしていたことについて，何度も批判しています．

I think that both candidates, Crooked Hillary and myself, should release detailed medical records. I have no problem in doing so! Hillary? (16:24 - 2016 年 8 月 28 日)

Using Alicia M in the debate as a paragon of virtue just shows that Crooked Hillary suffers from BAD JUDGEMENT! Hillary was set up by a con. (2:19 - 2016 年 9 月 30 日)

Crooked Hillary colluded w/FBI and DOJ and media is covering up to protect her. It's a #RiggedSystem! Our country deserves better! (14:03 - 2016 年 10 月 17 日)

Crooked Hillary should not be allowed to run for president. She deleted 33,000 e-mails AFTER getting a subpoena from U.S. Congress. RIGGED! (5:01 - 2016 年 11 月 1 日)

トランプ氏の tweet でよく現れる "Crooked Hillary" は，「不正なヒラリー」「ひねくれたヒラリー」という意味です．

5 討論会にて

アメリカ大統領選挙では 3 回にわたりテレビ討論会 (debate) がなされました[8]. ただ, 2 回目以降は具体的な政策論争よりもお互いの非難に終始し, 視聴者はうんざりしたようです. 以下, CLOSSTALK は「言い合い」です.

以下, 両者の討論を引用してみます. Twitter とは違い, トランプ氏は討論会で難しい単語を連発しています. 街頭演説や Twitter の言い回しは, 一般大衆向けにわかりやすくしたものと考えた方がよさそうです.

5.1 1 回目の討論会 (2016 年 9 月 29 日)

NBC Nightly News の Lester Holt 氏の司会で, ニューヨークの Hofstra University で行われました. この時はお互いに政策論争になりましたが, トランプ氏は気候変動（地球温暖化）は中国が広めたデマだと考えていると, クリントン氏が指摘したことに対し繰り返し否定しています.

TRUMP: I did not. I did not. I do not say that.
CLINTON: I think science is real.
TRUMP: I do not say that.

同じことを繰り返すことで強調しています. 次にトランプ氏は, クリントン元大統領が 1990 年代に NAFTA について, 批准することでアメリカ人に給料のいい雇用を創出するだろうと考えて支持したことを批判しています.

TRUMP: I will bring — excuse me. I will bring back jobs. You can't bring back jobs.
CLINTON: Well, actually, I have thought about this quite a bit.
TRUMP: Yeah, for 30 years.
CLINTON: And I have — well, not quite that long. I think my husband did a pretty good job in the 1990s. I think a lot about what worked and how we can make it work again...
TRUMP: Well, he approved NAFTA...
(CROSSTALK)
CLINTON: ... million new jobs, a balanced budget...

---

[8] NHK のニュースサイト
http://www3.nhk.or.jp/news/special/2016-presidential-election/index.html
などで全文と日本語訳が読めます. ただし, 日本語訳は一部省略されているところがあります

TRUMP: He approved NAFTA, which is the single worst trade deal ever approved in this country.

TRUMP: See, you're telling the enemy everything you want to do. No wonder you've been fighting — no wonder you've been fighting ISIS your entire adult life.

しまいには「自分が何をしたいか，敵に全て明かしてしまっている」とまでこき下ろしています．

次に納税申告書を公開していないという点を司会者から指摘された点の回答です．金額の生々しい話が現れた後のところを引用します．

TRUMP: Well, I told you, I will release them as soon as the audit. Look, I've been under audit almost for 15 years. I know a lot of wealthy people that have never been audited. I said, do you get audited? I get audited almost every year.

And in a way, I should be complaining. I'm not even complaining. I don't mind it. It's almost become a way of life. I get audited by the IRS. But other people don't.

I will say this. We have a situation in this country that has to be taken care of. I will release my tax returns — against my lawyer's wishes — when she releases her 33,000 e-mails that have been deleted. As soon as she releases them, I will release.

15 年ほど毎年監査 (audit) を受けており，一方で裕福 (wealthy) なのに監査を受けていない人を多く知っていると反論しています．国税庁 (IRS) の監査を受けているとも強調しています．そして，クリントン氏が削除した 33,000 通の電子メールを公開したら自分も納税申告書を公開すると反撃に出ました．

さらに納税についての反撃もあります．

I am very underleveraged. I have a great company. I have a tremendous income. And the reason I say that is not in a braggadocios way. It's because it's about time that this country had somebody running it that has an idea about money.

"underleveraged" は「負債の比率が低い」，"braggadocios" は「大ボラ吹き」という意味です．「お金について知っている人がこの国を運営するのがふさわしい」と，自分自身が次期大統領として適任としています．

その後，巨額の財政赤字について批判を強めます．

And it's really a shame. And it's politicians like Secretary Clinton that have caused this problem. Our country has tremendous problems. We're a debtor nation. We're a serious debtor nation. And we have a country that needs new roads, new tunnels, new bridges, new airports, new schools, new hospitals. And we don't have the money, because it's been squandered on so many of your ideas.

HOLT: We'll let you respond and we'll move on to the next segment.

CLINTON: And maybe because you haven't paid any federal income tax for a lot of years.

"debtor nation" は「負債国」です．国務長官として中東での施策がまずく，巨額の出費をしたことを批判しています．司会者の Holt 氏に促されたクリントン氏は，「あなたが連邦所得税 (federal income tax) を払っていないせいもあるかもしれない」と回答し，会場から拍手を浴びました．

地球温暖化は問題でないとしたトランプ氏は，核問題が唯一の問題であるとし，アメリカが様々な国を防衛しているのに，それらは相応の負担をしていないと批判しています．

Nuclear is the single greatest threat. Just to go down the list, we defend Japan, we defend Germany, we defend South Korea, we defend Saudi Arabia, we defend countries. They do not pay us. But they should be paying us, because we are providing tremendous service and we're losing a fortune. That's why we're losing – we're losing – we lose on everything. I say, who makes these – we lose on everything. All I said, that it's very possible that if they don't pay a fair share, because this isn't 40 years ago where we could do what we're doing. We can't defend Japan, a behemoth, selling us cars by the million...

"behemoth" はロールプレイングゲームなどに出てくるのでおなじみかもしれません．聖書「ヨブ記」に記載された「カバに似た巨獣」で，転じて「バケモノ」です．相応の負担をしないのに，何百万台もの自動車をアメリカに売りつける「バケモノ」を防衛できないと主張しているわけです[*9]．

5.2　2 回目の討論会 (2016 年 10 月 9 日)

セントルイスの Washington University で行われました．2 回目は対話集会形式で行われ，有権者が候補者に直接質問ができるようになっていました．

実はこの 2 回目の討論会の直前に，次章の『物議を醸したオフレコ』が公開され，質問が集中していたようです．CNN の Anderson Cooper 氏とのやりとりを抜粋します．

COOPER: We received a lot of questions online, Mr. Trump, about the tape that was released on Friday, as you can imagine. You called what you said locker room banter. You described kissing women without consent, grabbing their genitals. That is sexual assault. You bragged that you have sexually assaulted women. Do you understand that?
(註：次章とは異なる遠回しな言い回し "genitals"（生殖器，性器）を使っています)

[*9] 在日米軍駐留経費負担は以下を参照．
　　http://www.mod.go.jp/j/approach/zaibeigun/us_keihi/

"locker room banter" は「ロッカールームでの冗談」, "secual assalt" は「性的暴行」です.

TRUMP: No, I didn't say that at all. I don't think you understood what was – this was locker room talk. I'm not proud of it. I apologize to my family. I apologize to the American people. Certainly I'm not proud of it. But this is locker room talk.

You know, when we have a world where you have ISIS chopping off heads, where you have – and, frankly, drowning people in steel cages, where you have wars and horrible, horrible sights all over, where you have so many bad things happening, this is like medieval times. We haven't seen anything like this, the carnage all over the world.

And they look and they see. Can you imagine the people that are, frankly, doing so well against us with ISIS? And they look at our country and they see what's going on.

Yes, I'm very embarrassed by it. I hate it. But it's locker room talk, and it's one of those things. I will knock the hell out of ISIS. We're going to defeat ISIS. ISIS happened a number of years ago in a vacuum that was left because of bad judgment. And I will tell you, I will take care of ISIS.

「ロッカールームの冗談」だと説明した後, 突如 ISIS の残虐行為の話をして, ISIS を何とかすると話をそらしています. "hell out" は「叩きのめす」です.

COOPER: So, Mr. Trump...

TRUMP: And we should get on to much more important things and much bigger things.

COOPER: Just for the record, though, are you saying that what you said on that bus 11 years ago that you did not actually kiss women without consent or grope women without consent?

話が逸れたので, 司会者が 11 年前にバスの中で言ったように, 同意なしでキスしたり, 体を触ったり (grope) していないのか, 改めて問い直しています.

TRUMP: I have great respect for women. Nobody has more respect for women than I do.

COOPER: So, for the record, you're saying you never did that?

TRUMP: I've said things that, frankly, you hear these things I said. And I was embarrassed by it. But I have tremendous respect for women.

COOPER: Have you ever done those things?

TRUMP: And women have respect for me. And I will tell you: No, I have not. And I will tell you that I'm going to make our country safe. We're going to have borders in our country, which we don't have now. People are pouring into our country, and they're coming in from the Middle East and other places.

We're going to make America safe again. We're going to make America great again, but we're going to make America safe again. And we're going to make America wealthy again, because if you don't do that, it just – it sounds harsh to say, but we have to build up the wealth of our nation.

女性に敬意を持っていると述べた後,「この国を安全にする」と宣言し,国境 (border) を作るとまた話題が逸れていっているように見えます. そしてお決まりの "make America ... again" です.

さらに有権者からの質問に司会者からの質問が付け加わります.

RADDATZ: Jeff from Ohio asks on Facebook, "Trump says the campaign has changed him. When did that happen?" So, Mr. Trump, let me add to that. When you walked off that bus at age 59, were you a different man or did that behavior continue until just recently? And you have two minutes for this.

TRUMP: It was locker room talk, as I told you. That was locker room talk. I'm not proud of it. I am a person who has great respect for people, for my family, for the people of this country. And certainly, I'm not proud of it. But that was something that happened.

If you look at Bill Clinton, far worse. Mine are words, and his was action. His was what he's done to women. There's never been anybody in the history politics in this nation that's been so abusive to women. So you can say any way you want to say it, but Bill Clinton was abusive to women.

政治に目覚めたのがいつかという有権者からの質問に加えて,司会者の 59 歳(発言当時の年齢)の時にバスを降りた後,違う人間になったのか,それとも最近までこのような行動をとっていたのかと,皮肉を込めて問うています.

これに対し,トランプ氏は「ロッカールームでの冗談」と繰り返していますが,恥じているようです. ただ,自分は言葉だけだが,クリントン元大統領は行動をとったと批判しています. "abusive" は「虐待」です.

その後,トランプ氏はメールの問題で攻勢に出ます. 33,000 通もの電子メールを削除したことについて,厳しく追及しています.

TRUMP: If you did that in the private sector, you'd be put in jail, let alone after getting a subpoena from the United States Congress.

もし民間組織に属していて不適切なメールの取り扱いをしたならば,収監されるとし,連邦議会 (the United States Congress) から召喚状 (subpoena) を受けた後だったら,なおさらであると追及しています.

13

5.3 3回目の討論会 (2016 年 10 月 19 日)

ネバダ州の the University of Nevada, Las Vegas で行われました. Fox News の Chris Wallace 氏の司会で進められた最後の討論会は, お互いの中傷に終始した印象があります.

トピックは最高裁判所（銃規制, 妊娠中絶など）, 移民問題, 経済, 大統領の資質, 外国との紛争, 国の債務です. オバマケアが大失敗であると評するトランプ氏に対し, 富裕層への増税をして社会保障を手厚くするとクリントン氏が返し, ビジネスで多額の損失を被り所得税を 18 年間納めていなかったトランプ氏にを皮肉っています. *CLINTON: Well, Chris, I am on record as saying that we need to put more money into the Social Security Trust Fund. That's part of my commitment to raise taxes on the wealthy. My Social Security payroll contribution will go up, as will Donald's, assuming he can't figure out how to get out of it. But what we want to do is to replenish the Social Security Trust Fund...*

TRUMP: Such a nasty woman.

社会保障 (social security) の負担をしないことを批判しているわけです. これに対しトランプ氏が発言した nasty は「不快な, 意地の悪い, たちの悪い, 卑劣な」というような意味です. あっという間に流行語になり, ロゴ T シャツまで直ちに販売されたそうです.

もう一つ物議を醸した発言がもう一つあります. 司会者からの以下の問いかけに対する答えです.

WALLACE: Mr. Trump, I want to ask you about one last question in this topic. You have been warning at rallies recently that this election is rigged and that Hillary Clinton is in the process of trying to steal it from you.

Your running mate, Governor Pence, pledged on Sunday that he and you – his words – "will absolutely accept the result of this election." Today your daughter, Ivanka, said the same thing. I want to ask you here on the stage tonight: Do you make the same commitment that you will absolutely – sir, that you will absolutely accept the result of this election?

TRUMP: I will look at it at the time. I'm not looking at anything now. I'll look at it at the time.

司会者から, トランプ氏が集会 (rallies) でこの選挙が不正に操作 (rigged) されており, クリントン氏に票を盗まれていると発言したことが問われています. 副大統領候補の Pence 氏は「絶対に選挙結果を受け入れる」とし, トランプ氏の娘も同様に答えたとのことです. そこであえて司会者がトランプ氏に, 選挙結果を受け入れるかを問うたわけで

す．トランプ氏の返答の文章だけを出されたら意味がわかりませんが，「私はその時に考えるでしょう．今はそれについて何も考えていない．」という意味になります．負けた場合に選挙結果を受け入れないのではないかと疑われ，民主主義の根幹に関わる発言として問題になりました．

ところが，この件に関しても選挙後の tweet は相変わらずです．

The debates, especially the second and third, plus speeches and intensity of the large rallies, plus OUR GREAT SUPPORTERS, gave us the win! (10:46 - 2016 年 11 月 13 日)

6　物議を醸したオフレコ

ヒラリー・クリントン氏との果てしない中傷合戦では，クリントン氏の私用メール問題で FBI の調査が入るのではという一方で，トランプ氏のオフレコでの女性蔑視発言も物議を醸しました．ところが大手メディアはその詳細に触れようとしませんでした．その理由として，あまりに下品で卑猥すぎて，日本語に訳して報じるのが憚られる内容だったからと考えられます．

問題の発言は 2005 年，NBC の "Today" show に出演する際に，共演者の Billy Bush 氏との出演前に移動中のバスの中で行われたものです．Billy Bush は，ジョージ・ウォーカー・ブッシュ元大統領（息子の方です）の従兄弟です[*10]．ブッシュ元大統領も発言でいろいろありましたが，この従兄弟も如何なものかと思われます．避けて通るわけにもいかないので，New York Times で 2016 年 10 月 8 日に報じられた会話の内容を引用します[*11]．

Donald J. Trump: You know and ...

Unknown: She used to be great. She's still very beautiful.

Trump: I moved on her, actually. You know, she was down on Palm Beach. I moved on her, and I failed. I'll admit it.

Unknown: Whoa.

Trump: I did try and <u>fuck</u> her. She was married.
（彼女と<u>ヤろ</u>うとした．彼女は既婚者だった．）

Unknown: That's huge news.

Trump: No, no, Nancy. No, this was [unintelligible] — and I moved on her very heavily. In fact, I took her out furniture shopping.

She wanted to get some furniture. I said, "I'll show you where they have some

---

[*10] 父ブッシュは五男二女兄弟の次男．Billy Bush は四男の息子．

[*11] http://www.nytimes.com/2016/10/08/us/donald-trump-tape-transcript.html

nice furniture." I took her out furniture —

I moved on her like a bitch. But I couldn't get there. And she was married. Then all of a sudden I see her, she's now got the big phony <u>tits</u> and everything. She's totally changed her look.

（俺はアバズレのような女をナンパした．でもフラれたよ．彼女は既婚者だった．でも，その時彼女をみたらでかくて偽物の (phony) <u>オッパイ</u> だったよ．全く違う女に見えたよ.）

Billy Bush: Sheesh, your girl's hot as <u>shit</u>. In the purple.

Trump: Whoa! Whoa!

Bush: Yes! The Donald has scored. Whoa, my man!

[Crosstalk]

Trump: Look at you, you are a <u>pussy</u>.

（後半は「お前は女々しい！」というよりかなりキツイ言い回しです.）

[Crosstalk]

Trump: All right, you and I will walk out.

[Silence]

Trump: Maybe it's a different one.

Bush: It better not be the publicist. No, it's, it's her, it's —

Trump: Yeah, that's her. With the gold. I better use some Tic Tacs just in case I start kissing her. You know, I'm automatically attracted to beautiful — I just start kissing them. It's like a magnet. Just kiss. I don't even wait. And when you're a star, they let you do it. You can do anything.

（註："Tic Tacs" はミントタブレットです[*12].）

Bush: Whatever you want.

Trump: Grab 'em by the <u>pussy</u>. You can do anything.

（Grab'em は Grab them の簡略表現です．意味は英文の後に解説します.）

Bush: Uh, yeah, those legs, all I can see is the legs.

Trump: Oh, it looks good.

Bush: Come on shorty.

Trump: Ooh, nice legs, huh?

Bush: Oof, get out of the way, honey. Oh, that's good legs. Go ahead.

Trump: It's always good if you don't fall out of the bus. Like Ford, Gerald Ford, remember?

Bush: Down below, pull the handle.

Trump: Hello, how are you? Hi!

Arianne Zucker: Hi, Mr. Trump. How are you? Pleasure to meet you.

[*12] https://www.tictacusa.com/

Trump: Nice seeing you. Terrific, terrific. You know Billy Bush?

Bush: Hello, nice to see you. How you doing, Arianne?

Zucker: Doing very well, thank you. Are you ready to be a soap star?

下線を引いた単語は "four-letter words" とよばれる卑語とされるものです．アメリカでは 7 つの単語[13] が一律に放送禁止とされていました．これらは現在でも放送が憚られるようです．bitch は日本でも広まっているでしょう．元々は『雌犬』という意味ですが，『尻軽女，あばずれ女，性悪女』というような女性への悪口に使われることが多いです．男性に対しては son-of-a-bitch という表現で悪口に使われます．

さて，pussy は七大卑語ではありませんが，やはり放送が問題視される単語です．こちらの文の方が問題です．英和辞典ではまず『猫，子猫』などと出てきますが，そういう上品なものではありません．日本語としてあえて書くとすると，「おま○こ[14]を鷲づかみにできるぞ．スターならば何でもできるんだ．」というような，非常に下品な発言です．

なお，この会話に登場し，トランプ氏に負けず劣らず下品な発言をしている Billy Bush 氏は発言が発覚したのち，番組を降板させられています．

7　勝利宣言と勝利後の公約

2016 年 11 月 8 日の投票結果，トランプ氏は次期アメリカ大統領に選出されることとなりました．翌日に勝利宣言[15] をしていますが，単純な同じフレーズを繰り返すことで強調する意図を示しています．冒頭の部分を見てみましょう．

Thank you. Thank you very much, everyone. Sorry to keep you waiting. Complicated business, complicated. Thank you very much.

宣言全文で "thank you" は 16 回も出てきます．"Sorry to keep you waiting." は「長い間お待たせしたことをお詫びします」という意味です．

さて，トランプ氏にとって，まず進めなければならないことは，宣言の以下の部分でしょう．

I mean that very sincerely. Now it is time for America to bind the wounds of division, have to get together, to all Republicans and Democrats and independents across this nation I say it is time for us to come together as one united people.

---

[13] cocksucker, cunt, fuck, motherfucker, piss, shit, tits.

[14] 日本でもこの単語をテレビで発したことにより発言で漫画家の西原理恵子氏が番組降板，タレントの松本明子氏もしばらく干されました．ザ・タイマーズというロックバンドが突如歌詞を変えて生放送で歌った騒動がありますが，興味のある方はネット上でお調べください．

[15] 例えば以下のページに全文が掲載されています．
http://edition.cnn.com/2016/11/09/politics/donald-trump-victory-speech/index.html

It is time. I pledge to every citizen of our land that I will be president for all of Americans, and this is so important to me. For those who have chosen not to support me in the past, of which there were a few people, I'm reaching out to you for your guidance and your help so that we can work together and unify our great country. As I've said from the beginning, ours was not a campaign but rather an incredible and great movement, made up of millions of hard-working men and women who love their country and want a better, brighter future for themselves and for their family.

今回の大統領選挙はアメリカを分断するような騒動になってしまいました．選挙後もトランプ氏を次期大統領と認めない抗議デモが相次いでいます．2016 年 4 月にラッパーの Keenon Daequan Ray Jackson 氏（通称 YG）が "Fuck Donald Trump" という，トランプ氏を批判する曲を発表し，YouTube 上で 1000 万回以上再生されています[*16]．こちらもタイトルから想像できるように，fuck が数十回現れる過激な歌詞です．大きな分断を癒して一つにまとまるようにできるのか，今後の手腕が問われるところです．

勝利宣言では，今までのような放言に近い発言は控えているようです．もちろん強調しなければならないことはしっかり述べています．

Working together, we will begin the urgent task of rebuilding our nation and renewing the American dream. I've spent my entire life in business, looking at the untapped potential in projects and in people all over the world.

That is now what I want to do for our country. Tremendous potential. I've gotten to know our country so well. Tremendous potential. It is going to be a beautiful thing. Every single American will have the opportunity to realize his or her fullest potential. The forgotten men and women of our country will be forgotten no longer.

緊急課題 (urgent task) として，国を立て直しアメリカンドリームを新たに打ち立てることを宣言しています．利用されていない (untapped) 潜在能力を持つ事業や人々を，トランプ氏のビジネスキャリアで数多く見てきたというわけです．

周囲の国はハラハラしているようですが，ひとまず宣言では穏やかな発言に終始しています．

America will no longer settle for anything less than the best. We must reclaim our country's destiny and dream big and bold and daring. We have to do that. We're going to dream of things for our country, and beautiful things and successful things once again.

[*16] Part1: https://youtu.be/WkZ5e94QnWk
Part2: https://youtu.be/Jpg7Bj319oE

I want to tell the world community that while we will always put America's in-terests first, we will deal fairly with everyone, with everyone.

All people and all other nations. We will seek common ground, not hostility; partnership, not conflict. And now I would like to take this moment to thank some of the people who really helped me with this, what they are calling tonight a very, very historic victory.

外交に関しては，アメリカの利益を最優先にしつつも，どの国とも公平に付き合うということです．"hostility" は敵愾心 です．「歴史的な勝利の日となった」と言えるのは就任後の外交を見てみないとなんともいえないのではないでしょうか．

以下，数多くの人たちに対する謝辞が続きますので略します．勝利宣言は Twitter での tweet や，討論会での発言とは異なり，格調高い単語を散りばめています．トランプ氏の本音が見えるのは，Twitter や実際の発言の方ではないかと思われます．

また，公式サイトでは勝利宣言後に，有権者に対する公約を公表しています[17]．"Make America Great Again" を実現するための 100 日間の行動計画を示しています．有権者が名前を記入すれば，「トランプ氏との契約書」にサインする形になっています．NAFTA や TPP から離脱すること，国境に壁を作るなどという主張は相変わらず続けています．

8　大統領就任後の言動

選挙後もアメリカ国内では様々な抗議活動や，「公約」に対する疑義も多く続きました．例えば 2016 年 10 月 9 日，Lady Gaga 氏がニューヨークの Trump Tower の前で掲げたメッセージ

Love trumps hate.

は，なかなか意味深です．"trump" は「切り札，奥の手」という名刺の他に，「... に勝つ」「... を負かす」という他動詞でもあります．トランプ氏の名を使って，「愛は憎しみに勝つ」という分断した状況を揶揄しているようです[18]．

もしかしたら，第 26 代大統領 Theodore Roosevelt の名言

"The men with the muckrakers are often indispensable to the well being of society."
(醜聞を漁るもの (muckrakers) は，社会の福利にとってしばしば必要不可欠 (indispensable) である)

の通り，トランプ氏の醜聞がメディアによって次々漁られるのかもしれません．

しかし，2017 年 1 月 20 日に大統領に就任し，1 年以上が経過しました．ここからは，大統領就任後の言動を見ていきます．

---

[17] https://www.donaldjtrump.com/contract/
[18] 「トランプ氏大嫌い」と思いっきり誤訳した日本の放送局があったようです．

8.1 SNS で発表される閣僚人事

トランプ大統領の特徴は，閣僚の交代に関する人事を SNS で速報することです．

I had to fire General Flynn because he lied to the Vice President and the FBI. He has pled guilty to those lies. It is a shame because his actions during the transition were lawful. There was nothing to hide! (9:14 - 2017 年 12 月 2 日)

国家安全保障問題担当大統領補佐官に任命されていた，元陸軍中将のマイケル・フリン氏がロシア疑惑に関して副大統領と FBI に虚偽の供述をしたため，「クビにしなければならなかった」というわけです．NBC の番組「アプレンティス」で連呼した「You're fired（お前はクビだ）」を Twitter でも発言しています．

So General Flynn lies to the FBI and his life is destroyed, while Crooked Hillary Clinton, on that now famous FBI holiday "interrogation" with no swearing in and no recording, lies many times...and nothing happens to her? Rigged system, or just a double standard? (18:06 - 2017 年 12 月 2 日)

Mike Pompeo, Director of the CIA, will become our new Secretary of State. He will do a fantastic job! Thank you to Rex Tillerson for his service! Gina Haspel will become the new Director of the CIA, and the first woman so chosen. Congratulations to all! (5:44 - 2018 年 3 月 13 日)

CIA 長官のマイク・ポンペオ氏を国務長官に抜擢したという速報です．レックス・ティラーソン氏の更迭，ジーナ・ハスペル氏の CIA 長官（史上初の女性）選出も同時に発表しています．秘密工作部門で大半のキャリアを過ごし，経歴の詳細が謎に包まれているハスペル氏ですが，5 月 21 日に正式に CIA 長官に就任しています．相変わらず「ひねくれたヒラリー」と呼んでいます．"interrogation" は尋問のことです．"rigged" は不正操作されたという意味です．

8.2 中東問題

トランプ大統領の言動で混迷を深めている中東情勢ですが，特に 2017 年 12 月 6 日にエルサレムをイスラエルの首都と認め，アメリカ大使館を移転させるという演説は，大きな波紋を広げています[19]イスラエルは三権の機関をエルサレムに置いていますが，イス

---

[19] 演説に関する記事は
https://www.whitehouse.gov/briefings-statements/president-donald-j-trumps-proclamation-jerusalem-capital-state-israel/
にあります．

ラエルとパレスチナの対立の問題から，各国はイスラエルを首都と認めず，第二の都市テルアビブに大使館を置いています．アメリカは 1995 年に「エルサレム大使館移転法」を議会で可決していますが，パレスチナ情勢から移転には踏み切っていませんでした．ところがトランプ大統領が移転を決断しました．

...peace treaty with Israel. We have taken Jerusalem, the toughest part of the negotiation, off the table, but Israel, for that, would have had to pay more. But with the Palestinians no longer willing to talk peace, why should we make any of these massive future payments to them? (14:37 - 2018 年 1 月 2 日)

どちらかというとイスラエル寄りの発言に見えます．そしてイスラエル建国 70 周年に合わせて，アメリカ大使館をエルサレムで開館しました．

Big week next week when the American Embassy in Israel will be moved to Jerusalem. Congratulations to all! (16:39 - 2018 年 5 月 11 日)

U.S. Embassy opening in Jerusalem will be covered live on @FoxNews & @FoxBusiness. Lead up to 9:00 A.M. (eastern) event has already begun. A great day for Israel! (3:54 - 2018 年 5 月 14 日)

イランの核合意に関する破棄の背景についても，Twitter で言及しています．

Iran, the Number One State of Sponsored Terror with numerous violations of Human Rights occurring on an hourly basis, has now closed down the Internet so that peaceful demonstrators cannot communicate. Not good! (14:00 - 2017 年 12 月 31 日)

Iran is failing at every level despite the terrible deal made with them by the Obama Administration. The great Iranian people have been repressed for many years. They are hungry for food & for freedom. Along with human rights, the wealth of Iran is being looted. TIME FOR CHANGE! (4:44 - 2018 年 1 月 1 日)

イランは人権侵害を起こしているという再三にわたる非難をしています．

Iran's Military Budget is up more than 40% since the Obama negotiated Nuclear Deal was reached...just another indicator that it was all a big lie. But not anymore! (15:02 - 2018 年 5 月 12 日)

オバマ大統領の核合意から軍事費が 40% 以上上がっているということを指摘しています．中東情勢の今後が気になるところです．

8.3 ロケットマン→金正恩

史上初の米朝首脳会談がどうなるか，世界中が注目していました．この件も二転三転しました．

大統領就任直後の発言では，ミサイル実験を繰り返す金正恩に対し「ロケットマン」を連呼しています．

I spoke with President Moon of South Korea last night. Asked him how Rocket Man is doing. Long gas lines forming in North Korea. Too bad! (4:53 - 2017 年 9 月 17 日)

Just heard Foreign Minister of North Korea speak at U.N. If he echoes thoughts of Little Rocket Man, they won't be around much longer! (20:08 - 2017 年 9 月 23 日)

Being nice to Rocket Man hasn't worked in 25 years, why would it work now? Clinton failed, Bush failed, and Obama failed. I won't fail. (12:01 - 2017 年 10 月 1 日)

実は金正恩を「ロケットマン」呼ばわりしていたのは，ここまでです．これ以降は以下のように「金正恩」と呼んでいます．

North Korean Leader Kim Jong Un just stated that the "Nuclear Button is on his desk at all times." Will someone from his depleted and food starved regime please inform him that I too have a Nuclear Button, but it is a much bigger & more powerful one than his, and my Button works! (16:49 - 2018 年 1 月 2 日)

The highly anticipated meeting between Kim Jong Un and myself will take place in Singapore on June 12th. We will both try to make it a very special moment for World Peace! (7:37 - 2018 年 5 月 10 日)

2018 年 6 月 12 日に米朝首脳会談をシンガポールで行う予定だったのですが，その直前の 5 月 24 日にトランプ大統領が突然，中止表明を行いました[20]．その際に，トランプ大統領は同日での開催が復活する可能性を匂わせています．

We are having very productive talks with North Korea about reinstating the Summit which, if it does happen, will likely remain in Singapore on the same date, June 12th., and, if necessary, will be extended beyond that date. (17:37 - 2018 年 5 月 25 日)

---

[20] 中止表明の書簡は
https://www.whitehouse.gov/briefings-statements/letter-chairman-kim-jong-un/
で見ることができます．

結局，会談をシンガポールで行うことになりました．

Our United States team has arrived in North Korea to make arrangements for the Summit between Kim Jong Un and myself. I truly believe North Korea has brilliant potential and will be a great economic and financial Nation one day. Kim Jong Un agrees with me on this. It will happen! (13:09 - 2018 年 5 月 27 日)

会談の成果が大きかったとトランプ大統領はつぶやいています．

A year ago the pundits & talking heads, people that couldn't do the job before, were begging for conciliation and peace - "please meet, don't go to war." Now that we meet and have a great relationship with Kim Jong Un, the same haters shout out, "you shouldn't meet, do not meet!" (18:14 - 2018 年 6 月 12 日)

Just landed - a long trip, but everybody can now feel much safer than the day I took office. There is no longer a Nuclear Threat from North Korea. Meeting with Kim Jong Un was an interesting and very positive experience. North Korea has great potential for the future! (2:56 - 2018 年 6 月 13 日)

ここで現れた "pundits" は，賢者，専門家，権威者という意味の難しい単語です．ホワイトハウスの公式サイトでも，今回の米朝首脳会談を「歴史的な会談」と評して，肯定的に報じたニュースをまとめて掲載しています[*21]．会談の成果は今後の情勢を見ないとわからないでしょう．

8.4　covfefe – 謎のつぶやき

トランプ大統領は Twitter を使っていろいろな発言をしていますが，一番の謎とされるつぶやきはこれです．

Despite the constant negative press covfefe. (2017 年 5 月 31 日 - 5:06)

この "covfefe" とは一体何だろうかと，様々な憶測を呼びました．大統領選を争ったヒラリー・クリントンは以下のように皮肉っています．*People in covfefe houses shouldn't throw covfefe.* (2017 年 6 月 1 日 - 10:30)

"people in glass houses shouldn't throw stones." 「ガラスの家の住民は石を投げるべきではない」の単語を置き換えています．ロシアの協力を得て大統領に就任したという疑惑があり，「ロシアへの秘密のメッセージではないか」という憶測もありました．結局のところ，トランプ大統領はこのツイートを削除し，以下のように文章を置き換えています．

[*21] https://www.whitehouse.gov/briefings-statements/historic-summit-north-korea-tremendous-moment-world/

Who can figure out the true meaning of "covfefe" ??? Enjoy! (2017 年 5 月 31 日 - 19:09)

おそらく "coverage" のタイプミスではないかと考えられていますが，大統領のツイートを誰もチェックしていないのではないかという懸念が生じています．

この動きを受けて，民主党のマイク・クイグリー下院議員は 6 月 12 日，大統領の SNS などへの投稿を公文書として保管することを義務付ける法案を議会に提出しています．この法案は "Communications Over Various Feeds Electronically for Engagement Act"（多様な電子的手段による職務上の通信法）で，略すと "COVFEFE 法" になります．

9 おわりに

大統領に選出されたトランプ氏の英文はいかがでしたでしょうか．わかりやすいフレーズで人々の心を掴んだと思われるでしょう．ただ，内容は顔をしかめるようなものではないかと思います．過激な発言を繰り返してきましたが，これらの公約は果たして実現できるのでしょうか．それとも公約をうやむやにしたり，あるいは任期途中に辞任に追い込まれるような事態になるのでしょうか[22]．

日朝首脳会談がうまくまとまれば，ノーベル平和賞受賞の可能性も言及されていますが，決裂した場合には武力行使の可能性もゼロでは無いだけに，今後の言動が気になるところです．世界を平和に導いた偉大な大統領となるのか，それとも世界を大混乱に陥れた大統領となるのか，いずれにせよ少なくとも世界の歴史には大きな名を残すでしょう．

トランプ氏に学ぶ英語表現

2016 年 11 月 20 日 初版 発行
2018 年 8 月 12 日 改訂版 発行
2024 年 12 月 16 日 増刷

著　者	茗荷 さくら （みょうが さくら）
発行者	星野 香奈 （ほしの かな）
発行所	同人集合 暗黒通信団 （https://ankokudan.org/d/）
	〒277-8691 千葉県柏局私書箱 54 号 D 係
本　体	200 円 / ISBN978-4-87310-060-9 C0082

Σ∞　乱丁・落丁は在庫がある限りお取り替えいたします．

© Copyright 2016–2024 暗黒通信団　　　Printed in Japan

---

[22] 任期途中で辞任したアメリカ大統領は，第 37 代の Richard Milhous Nixon だけです．日本の首相とは大きく異なります．